God Wants You to Smile Today ☺

25 Epiphanies of God's Goodness
Secrets to Living with Radical Peace, Joy, and Hope

Jeremy Holloway

God Wants You to Smile Today

Copyright © 2018 Jeremy Holloway

All Rights Reserved.

I want to thank my wife and acknowledge

my two kiddos, Asher and Anaya.

I love you guys so much!

Strength and dignity are her clothing, and she smiles at the future. Proverbs 31:25

Table of Contents

Introduction

A Little Bit About Me

I'm a boy from Toledo, Ohio, who grew up in the 80s, when Michael Jackson's "Beat It" dominated the radio. I still remember third grade wearing my biker pants and Michael Jackson's trademark black jacket! All my life, even back then, I was always a fan of three things: God, music, and education. I've always been intrigued with how things work, but especially how God is good, great, and how He works in our lives. I graduated from the University of Toledo in Education, and have loved teaching ever since.

Now what is an Epiphany? The dictionary defines Epiphany as "a sudden perception of the essential nature or being of God." I believe we all have epiphanies from time to time. I remember growing up eating hot delicious pancakes and listening to my dad as he would share with me the wonderful things that God had done for our family. He often shared with us the realizations and the epiphanies of God's awesomeness and His love. Now, since I, like my father, love hearing and telling the epiphanies we have about God's goodness, I thought, "Why not share the things I love with others!"

In this book, I will share with you the messages and light-bulb-over-the-head "A-ha!" moments in my life that illuminated the goodness and greatness of God alone, of God with us, and of God in my life. Let's get on with this!

God Smiles?

Smile on me. Psalm 31:16a

When my daughter was four months old, she had two types of smiles: one was after she had a great nap and the second was after she had eaten one of mom's nice and tasty meals. How could we fully translate those smiles? Her smile just lit up the room. As we grow up, we smile for multiple reasons, but the wonder of a smile, I believe, never goes away. God wants us to smile like my little girl every day. So what is a smile?

I believe a smile is more than a pleased or amused facial expression on our face. Here's my definition: "A smile is a silent shout of joy that expresses who we really are and who we were meant to be for eternity." It shows who God is and is a glimpse of what God has in store for you. Whoever you are. Whatever your job is. There is a part of you that beckons to bring delight and joy to others, and it's God who gives you that beckoning feeling. It is effortless to bring joy to others, and it is your calling.

Regardless of Bill Gates's stand on religion, he had a simple idea to create desktop computers. Some may think he pursued this because perhaps it was a way to make more money. I would argue that. Instead, Mr. Gates saw a way that he could put a smile on the faces of those he cared about and spread that smile throughout mankind. Just recently, I read a book about a man who said his sole purpose of doing his work was just because he enjoyed seeing the smile on people's faces when they used something that he created. A smile is important. Your smile is important.

You were made to make people smile.

I personally believe that when you make someone smile, you are stronger than Superman. You are a greater genius than Einstein. You display more ingenuity than the architects of the tallest skyscrapers of our time. With one flinch of your talents, worlds of people are changed. One spark of your inspiration makes people nod their heads with gratitude, wondering how you did it. Without effort, you can build up, strengthen, and encourage an entire nation. You were made to make people smile.

God Himself smiles, and He smiles on you TODAY.

The Lord will bless you and watch over you.
*The Lord will **smile** on you and be kind to you.*
The Lord will look on you with favor and give you peace.
(Numbers 6:24-26)

We know from Genesis that in the beginning God created the heavens and the earth. We smile when we see a flower. What do we think God's expression was when He created the heavens? When He created the earth? When He created YOU? When He breathed the breath of life into YOUR life? When He created the world, He smiled. When He created the flowers of the field, He smiled. When He created you, our God sang a song that said, "Be fruitful and multiply! "God smiles at you and He wants you to smile as well. Think about when Jesus raised Lazarus from the dead. How many smiles were resurrected from just that one event?

God already smiles upon you. You are accepted. When you were born, God smiled. God sees all the things He has for you in your future, and He smiles with joy and delight. This can be strange for us to think about, but I encourage you to think of it until it becomes a normal part of your thoughts. God smiles with full love and acceptance at you today.

Facts and fears.

Your talents are facts; we are to view them as such. What do I mean by saying our talents are facts? I mean that they ought to be viewed with a sense of worth, of truth, of value, and something unquestionable. We should look at them and study them as if we read a textbook or a nonfiction book, as if God made them, because He did. The kind of fear that is unproductive in our lives is to be viewed as fiction, in the sense that they can be manipulated. We often make the mistake of viewing our talents without a sense of value, and viewing our fears as though they are fact. But in the long run this is not productive viewing. Let's take a moment to look at talent around us. Look around you today. The stroke of genius in a butterfly as the butterfly flutters, in the song of a song bird, the intricacies of a tree in the forest, in a swan flying over a pond, in the birth of a newborn child. They are all facts, reality, pure truth, and unquestionable; but how did they happen? Was it genius? They seem so natural. The truth is that all of these are genius, but how it happens, with such ease and effortlessness, results in fear being the last thing we think of when we witness it. It is exactly this way with you, who you are, and with your natural talents. Don't think about your fears, but instead think of the things that simply come natural to you, the kind of things you do that naturally make other people smile. Think of this: Does a chick need a degree to learn how to get out of the egg? Not at all! Did a lion need to study to be king of the jungle? No way! Hard work, study, and college degrees are all well deserving of great achievements. However, they do not define the fact that so many of the natural, pure, and uplifting talents you already have represent what you are and have always been made to do. Don't let anyone downplay your uplifting talents. Instead, know that you were made to do whatever it is that you do!

The fact is that you were born with your dream job. It was laid inside of you even before you were born. God said to the prophet Jeremiah, *Before I formed you in the womb, I knew you, I appointed you to be a prophet to the nations (Jeremiah 1:5)*. There is not a human being on the face of this planet who has not been called to a very specific purpose, just as specific as your signature or your DNA. We have to be careful when we downplay what sets us apart and what has always been positively uplifting and inspiring for others through our lives.

Your talents are no mystery. Others may notice your talents before you do because you will see their genuine smile looking at you, and they will see the smile you have when you use your talents. Don't say that you don't have any special talent, and don't believe others who tell you that you are talentless. You were made! Think about it! YOU WERE MADE! You are here! Welcome! Here you are! You do not just fill up space. You were made to change and upwardly curve faces! Look carefully and examine the smiles and strokes of genius in your life. Each and every one of your talents are marks of God's genius, and remember that just as you smile, they make God smile. So use them. Your marks of genius do the same. Your ideas, laughter, and joyful duties brought on by God Himself make God smile. God wants to smile! God is not looking for things that make Him upset. He is looking for those who will put a smile on His face. And guess what? He's looking at you today! That is why He wants us to smile! God is a smiler! When you show your talents, you show the kind of genius that no other person can duplicate. That's genuine. And genuine talent produces genuine smiles. Amen to that!

Being yourself: How God wants you to believe in yourself in a way that honors God.

When I was growing up, the word "self" was like a cuss word. I remember thinking it was like a sin to be about "self." And needless to mention, I thought that "believing in yourself" was sacrilegious. But I've learned that "self" in and of itself, is not a cuss word, and believing in oneself is not bad and it all relates to context. For example, did Jesus believe that He was who He said He was? That's a silly question isn't it? Now, let me ask you: Do you believe that you are who God says you are? Do you believe that you are who Jesus says you are? That is the "self" you need to be, and the "self" you need to strongly believe in. Jesus says, *"You are the light of the world" (Matthew 5:14a).* Do you believe this? Do you take this seriously? Do you talk like you believe this? When you believe in what God is doing in your life, you are giving yourself permission to be yourself, and to be the person God says you are to others. Are you believing in the person that God made you to be? God says you are generous, kind, compassionate, patient, and joyful. Things are the qualities that can come out of our lives, which can make many people around us smile. So believe, but remember to believe in God over yourself because you are in such desperate need of Him. We are all like little sheep without a shepherd. We are all in need of God, and we need to believe in what He can do in our lives.

There are two ways to view the phrase, "Believe in yourself." One way is to see yourself as the first (and, perhaps, only) source of strength and power. This, of course, is an incorrect view for one to have in oneself because we are not as powerful as the One who created us. The other way, the way I am referring to, is a healthy way to view ourselves:

as people made in the image of God and called to a specific purpose.

Let's get to the point. When you are yourself, the person who God called on you to be, you make people smile. Take the time you need. You may need longer than a day or so, but take the time and learn about who you are and who God made you to be. Don't think too hard about it. If you are wondering about this area of your life, I suggest just going for a walk with your Bible and discuss it with God. I'm here to remind you that you are an amazing and wondrous child of God Most High. Think of those who have conquered cities, those who ruled as kings, those who brought people to tears of joy as they performed musically or with another inspiring talent before thousands. When you smile, you are doing more than that! Here is another marvelous work, a word that God spoke to me in prayer, "Obedience and patience to let God unfold before you who He made you to be is also a marvelous work." When you are being yourself, you are better than a man who takes over a city. *Better a patient person than a warrior, one with self-control than one who takes a city (Proverbs 16:32).*

Take the time you need and examine the times when you genuinely smiled. Log these moments in your journal and pray for God to reveal to you more opportunities. As your heart opens to His work in all the areas of your life, lift these moments up to Him. Ask God, "Lord, in what areas of my life do you want me to smile? I give those over to You. Lord, the areas that I make other people smile, I step boldly into those and ask that You bless those moments and grant me the confidence to continue walking in them as You reveal Yourself, Your word, and who You are to me."

The courage to smile

There are times in our lives when it is definitely harder to smile. I have experienced these myself. As a child I was made fun of a lot for being overweight, and it was sometimes hard just to go to school. It made me think, "I did not do anything to these people," and I wondered why they were doing these things to put me down. At some point, I decided that I would not be overweight for the rest of my life. I started to lift heavy cans in my room and jog in place for 30 minutes each day while I watched an episode of the Simpsons. I remember doing abdominal crunches with my mom and sisters on the weekends. It was very hard, but today it gives me incredible delight to make others smile with the story of overcoming. You, too, are an overcomer! I'd like to say that means that you aren't, won't, and didn't do it because of the obstacles, but instead you are the one who did it despite the obstacles!

What are the things you need to do to get out of the muck and make thousands of people smile? Write down some things, or contact me at Jeremy.holloway@utoledo.edu. You can also find me at jeremyholloway.com. I would like to hear both your story and your challenges, and see if there is anything I can do to help you out. God bless you.

Chapter One

God Smiles at Your Purpose

My soul yearns, even faints,
for the courts of the Lord;
my heart and my flesh cry out
for the living God.
Psalm 84:2

Epiphany #1: Eternity in Our Hearts

Are you searching? Look into your heart. Wait a moment...did you catch that? Look first in your heart when you are looking for something? All of the answers for your life's direction must start there! *Be still and know that He is God (Psalm 46:10)*. Remember and know that eternity and your heart are woven fearfully together. Here, my use of "fearfully" comes from the Psalms, where David said, *"I am fearfully and wonderfully made" (Psalm 139:14)*. That means that we were remarkably made by God. Our hearts were remarkably made. Perhaps this is why no person can know the heart, and why God looks so deeply into our hearts and searches each one. Perhaps this is why we are wise to be careful and vigil to the condition of our hearts, and what we place or bestow thereof.

It is in the heart, not in the world, where God speaks to us intimately. He speaks in the language of our hearts. This language is His Word. His eternal words of life, and the spiritual blood our hearts yearn for His Word each and every day.

Epiphany #2: The most wonderful place in the universe

What would the most wondrous place be for God? I mean, if God could go anywhere in the world and stay there forever, where would it be? What a profound secret place this would be! This place would beat out any other place in this world! In fact, I would say in this entire universe. Where is this place? The heart. The heart is where He speaks to us. No place on earth has anything on this. Forget Las Vegas!

Forget Disneyland! Disneyland is fun. But God doesn't need Space Mountain. The heart is where it all happens.

This is where God's word is ever growing, living, and breathing. God breathes into the secret places of your heart. Our heart also tells us to speak to God. *My heart says of you, 'Seek his face!' Your face, LORD, I will seek (Psalm 27:8).*

Let's ask God to speak and move in our hearts today. As we read His word today, let us open our hearts and ask God to work powerfully in our hearts through this book. Be open to speaking with Him in unconventional ways. Talk to Him like you would a friend through this book. My hope is that this book will not just give you nice fuzzy feelings, but that this book will empower you to move with whatever God has called you to do from your heart and in your life today. *His word will be a lamp to our feet and a light to our path (Psalm 119:105),* and we should open our hearts and pray for one another right now.

Epiphany #3: You are born with purpose

You were born with purpose. You are born with uniqueness. *You are fearfully and wonderfully made (Psalm 139:14).* You were made incredibly unique and never made to fit into something the world had made before. Unique is who you are and how you were made to function. That uniqueness, you must understand, has only one purpose, and that is to SHINE like the sun. Not hide, but SHINE! Be who you were made to be.

Think of how a star shines its light. It comes from intense pressure and temperature at the core. From the core, the atoms of hydrogen are fused into atoms of helium and the reaction releases a great amount of energy that causes a star to shine. In the same way, you were made to shine, and the dreams and visions are sitting there inside your heart. Don't be afraid to look into your heart and find those dreams and visions. Your purpose on this earth may be determined by the amount of pressure and difficulties that may come from moving forward with your Godly purpose. We should be wise, but perhaps it's that very pressure that will make you shine your light in this world.

Wouldn't it be sad if the sun shied away from its brightness? Would it continue to be a star? An even better question is: would we ever want the sun to be shy about its brightness? For obvious reasons, not at all! If the sun didn't shine, the earth would lose all its beauty and life. But we also wouldn't want the sun to be any brighter for the exact same reasons. There is a balance and there is a target. It is the same with us, our gifts, and our uniqueness in this world. A cold world is the result from a lack of sun shining on it. We need a relationship with God daily because He birthed our purpose and it has been with us since (and before) we were born. Walk with God and ask Him about your purpose. Speak with Him about it today.

Think of how you can shine your God-given, smile-inducing uniqueness to this world! You know your gifts better than you may realize. Think of how you have encouraged others in this world. For example, when I was in the second grade, I remember drawing one picture of a character from a 1980s cartoon, and to my surprise, one student took notice of it and advertised my drawing to the entire classroom. It totally changed my life, and from that point onward I knew that I was good at drawing. I knew because I loved drawing and it encouraged others to draw.

Think of some events when this happened for you. Begin creating these experiences by joining a small group doing something you are interested in. If you cannot find a group, make one yourself. You can get the ball rolling on something that's not only good for you, but for those around you. Do not rob yourself of the opportunity to have this experience today! It takes activity to get moving!

The words Jesus spoke, *"You are the light of the world"* *(Matthew 5:14)*, can be interpreted as, "You are My revealed purpose, the purpose of God revealed in the world." You are His art! You are His heart! You are the blazing light, and your talents, dreams, and ambitions are the light that gives heat and light to this world - and His Word ignites it! "Don't you dare stop!" is what I'm saying! You were not made just to be unique. You are unique, and through Christ, you bring good that we cannot express (or even pronounce) with our phonetic language. In this way, we are a blazing, bright fire for this world. So take action! Shine your God-given talents and gifts. Think of ways you can inspire this nation, one person at a time. Write them down right now.

The power of a smile

I remember my first mission trip to Managua, Nicaragua. At the time, I did not know the language, and honestly, I didn't even know where Nicaragua was on the map! I remember being excited about the warm weather because it was January, and January in northern Ohio can be pretty brutal with its cold temperatures. The tropical air was so refreshing to me because it was my first time ever to be warm while standing outside in the middle of January.

We were in Managua to help build a church from the ground up. I recall seeing the welcoming smiles from those who welcomed us. I remember trying to speak with the individuals who we served. I could not speak a word of Spanish, but I could tell by the expressions on each person's face that they appreciated having us there. I didn't know the language, but their smiles were all the communication that I needed. I think in fact, only seeing their smiles in a way gives more power and authenticity to the experience. I've studied how times like this can often bring us back to those good times when we were babies, when smiling expressions on faces really meant something to us because it was the way we communicated the most with others. You could say that at that moment, I experienced grace through the innate senses because of these people. And I can still see their faces now.

Since then, I have met other people who have been on a mission trip or have taken trips to serve in relief projects. They have said the same thing. They often say that it was their intent to travel and serve the people they came to visit, but in fact it was they themselves who felt served by the people there. They remember the faces of the individuals and how they made them feel. They remember the smiles on their faces, and it made a deep impact in their lives. Those smiles had a great impact on their lives, and I'm sure the feeling was likewise. I believe deep down inside that we are all called to make someone else smile. There's power in a smile. There is power when you give a smile to someone else. There is power when you receive a smile from someone. And there is great power when know that your life caused someone else to smile genuinely. I believe that is our own life's purpose. It seems simple, but I have experienced that there is great, great satisfaction from making someone else smile. I believe that this is not only our calling, but a sure way that we can discover our calling even if we don't know exactly what it is. We were all called to make someone else smile with our lives. Can you look back at times when you made someone else smile? Perhaps when you were at the supermarket? Or at your job? Or maybe while you were playing an instrument, or sports, or simply walking outside. I'm sure they were blessed as well. Think of these things, and reflect on these things before you go to bed. These little things often make up a big part of what life's all about. How do you see yourself making other people smile?

Epiphany #4: Grab a vision!

Dare to close your eyes, pray, and see yourself at the end of this year. Where do you want to see yourself in another 365 days? Smiling, grateful, and surrounded by people who love you and believe in you? I'd say yes to all of that. I'm going to believe with you. Trust that God is guiding you every step of the way. Do not dare be paralyzed. Do not justify not moving forward. You can be still and know He is God as you ask Him, seek after Him, and knock on His front door, so to speak. Know that God is there with you and He has opened the door. Now it's up to us to move forward and walk through it.

Your destiny is right in front of you today. But the open door may seem to be very small or insignificant. So trust God. He has your destiny with you right now. He is positioning you for success. He's already there in your future waiting for you to take that step in faith. Start to receive God's gentle pull towards your destiny and push yourself towards it. Your destiny has two parts: God's pull and your push toward it. But the push and pull can be slowed down by distractions. God is always pulling you towards your destiny. When you feel like you're getting distracted, stop and wait on God. Pray and ask God for silence. Be still and get to know God more.

Let me say this again: God is always pulling you towards your destiny. Something may look good, or even logically make sense, but God may be calling you towards a direction that He knows so much better. That is the vision for you. We have to be careful what we are pushing towards; that is why we need God. His pull is the place where we push. Stop and look to see where God is blessing our efforts. We are always pushing, but it's always in the wrong direction if it is not from God. I promise you that your vision for your life is here right now with you, but you must listen to God.

Your destiny could be right in front of you in the form of a seed, but in order to know which seed is the one to grow 100 fold, begin to ask God. Trust that He is pulling you in that direction, and once all the other seeds are scattered and gone, it will all make complete sense because He made you for this season, for this reason.

Let's pray this prayer together: "God, guide my heart towards Your pull. God push me towards Your pull. God, if Your name's not in it, then God, I drop it. And I pick up things You've given to me. ONLY the things You've given to me, Lord I take. In Jesus' name. Amen.

Chapter Two

God Smiles on You with Love

Epiphany #5: God So Loved Us

*"For God so loved the world that He gave His only begotten
Son, that whoever believes in Him should not perish but
have everlasting life." John 3:16*

Think of God. Now think of the universe. Compare the size of a single thought in your mind about anything to the size of the universe. Now think of God and His love again. In awe, ponder the massiveness of God and His holiness. God is big, but He cares about your thoughts more than the entire universe. Size is not a factor to God. God stamps His words "holy" and "glory" in and over our hearts.

God's faithfulness is incomparable to anything we have ever seen or can ever imagine (see Ephesians 3:20 and Psalm 136:1). His faithfulness is holy. There is nothing on this earth like His faithfulness. God created the stars, and yet with us, He so loved. Think of that! That means the universe is too small to hold His love for us. God Himself so loved. God, who doesn't have to answer to any man, SO loves us. GOD. All-Powerful. All-Knowing. Unfathomable in glory, splendor and holiness. God so loves us.

The word "so" is fascinating to me. This word "so" is like an expression of immeasurable love. It is inexpressible how much God loves us. That is why God Himself came to earth and, with holy passion, died for all of us on the cross. Ponder the massiveness of the universe. Now picture a spot so small that it cannot be seen with the naked eye. That is the universe in comparison to the size of God's love for us. The universe is smaller than a spot compared to God's love for us!

There were times in my life when God revealed to me that He loves me, and I don't need to work so super hard to earn his love and trust. God loves us even if we don't work for it. God loves us in the moments when we may not even love Him. One of the ways I experienced God's love was through my dear wife, Kayla. I was struggling in my life, feeling like Peter on the boat, fishing for fish and left without even a small tuna fish! It was when I gave up and let God take care of that part in my life when Kayla showed up right there in front of me! It was amazing! I laughingly tell her I feel like Peter with the angel guiding me out of the jail and thinking, "Is this a dream?" It's not, and neither is it for you! I encourage you to let go and to trust God. Trust that God loves you and that He is taking care of you.

Now say to yourself aloud, "God SO LOVES ME!" Yell it if you have to! It is important for us to hear ourselves say these things about who God made us to be. The spoken word is so powerful - God created everything, all beginning with a spoken word, "And God said, 'Let there be light,' and there was light" (Genesis 1:3). God so shows me His goodness, God so gives to me all I need. In all His goodness, God so declares His glory in and through me, and through His Son. God so reveals His faithfulness to me. God so fills my heart today. I am so blessed today. He has opened up every possibility in my life. The Lord God of more than enough.

I believe that He has brought much for us today. We need to, with passion and with a crazy positive attitude, believe that today, whether we see it or not. God is "so" for you and for me because He has spoken it to you today.

Epiphany #6: God and His love for us are more good than we can imagine.

Now to him who is able to do immeasurably more than all we ask or imagine, according to his power that is at work within us. Ephesians 3:20

I love movies. I love watching the battles of action heroes who come to the rescue and save the strange planet from a group of very eccentric traders from a faraway galaxy. I think movies are the coolest. I love biographical movies the most because these life story movies seem to be inspired by God Himself.

Those biographies are just so amazing because, you know, as the category implies, it's factual. I love the stories about great figures in our history, such as Mother Teresa and Martin Luther King Jr. The stories are so moving. I mean, who wouldn't like their story? What was it that caused these individuals to have such a conviction? I believe that they knew something about God that they wanted to communicate to people. They wanted to express the secret that isn't really a secret at all – that God is so much more good than we could ever think of or imagine. God proves in our hearts, daily, that He is so much better than what we could ever dream or imagine.

The problem is we have our own limitations, and that is why we need God. That is why we need God's word to show us how great this life is, and how great is our God. God's grace and His goodness abound in us every day. It abounds today like never before because God loves to be with us in the present, here and now.

Those negative thoughts telling us that God is not moving in your life right now is a lie straight from satan. Don't believe the enemy's lies that today God is doing less than what He was doing in your life yesterday. No. God is working. I'm telling you, it's much more. Whether you see it or not, God is moving in your life *today* – you just don't see it yet. Remember, God is making something out of you in your life today that is so big you are going to look back and laugh in amazement to see what God has done (See John 5:17). Trust Him.

For it is God who works in you to will and to act in order to fulfill his good purpose. Philippians 2:13

Chapter Three

God Made You High Quality, so Smile

Epiphany #7: God doesn't make low quality days! God makes quality people and quality days! You are quality! High quality!

Today is the day that the Lord has made; let's rejoice and be glad in it. Psalm 118:24

I'm sure you've heard of the labels we give our regular weekdays: "Monday, Monday…" "Terrible Tuesday…" "Hump Day Wednesday!…" Well, think about it, what did these days ever do to us, huh? We call Monday what she is before she even arrives! That's not fair! Remember, who is more important: a day, or you, who God made the day for? In God's eyes, you are more important. God heard Joshua and He made the sun stand still. Why did God do that?

Because He loves His people and He wanted to fight for Israel; Joshua was a guy who knew that. I'm telling you, God loves you exactly like He loves Joshua. We can take from this that God values us greatly and, with the right heart, God places great value to our words (that means, He *listens* to us).

A day can't and doesn't speak, obviously. But you can, and you are more important than a day. So I encourage you to steer the day. The day is like the horse. You are the rider. Would a rider ever ask the horse where they want to go? No. Rather, the rider has a clear idea, and passionately directs the horse where to go. It is the same thing with your day. Tell your day how blessed it is. Speak to God in the morning and then steer the day. That means you can call a day what it is, and the day has to listen to you just as well! So I suggest we call this day blessed! Who's with me?

"This is the day the Lord has made, I will rejoice and be glad in it!" Psalm 118:24

Remember this: God doesn't make any low-quality days. He only makes the best of quality, higher than the highest that we can fathom, anything that we can possibly think of as a highest quality. Every day is full of high quality by

God's standards. This is beyond our imaginations, but even though, we can still fully enter into this high-quality day.

Knowing that all the days that God makes are high quality, David the giant-slayer once said, *"This is the day that the Lord has made. I will rejoice and be glad in it!" (Psalm 118:24).* Another translation of rejoice is, "be full of joy." How do we enter into a high quality day? We alert every fiber of our being, and we tell them to be full of joy! We create high expectations, knowing that the day is capable of bringing our dreams into light! A high quality person is demonstrated here. The day is already high quality from sunup to sundown in EVERY way because the LORD hath made it! Now ALL we have to do to take part in this day is Rejoice and be glad. Get excited and expect supernatural things to happen! A high quality person is one who rejoices and learns - yes that's right - *learns* how to be glad! They are those who are content with being content, and are glad with being glad. This is out of habit. Not because of the lottery. Not because somebody patted them on the back. Just because of what God has already done for them, His love for us. O taste and see that the Lord is good! Great are His words. *Sweeter than honey are your words, God! (Psalm 119:103).*

Every habit is the same: hard to start, but easier with repetition. I want to challenge you to start the habit of challenging your own perspectives on each day. There are days that don't seem to be the best of quality. There are days when things do not go as we planned, and they seem at the moment to go for the worst. I do not want to undermine real challenges and problems we may have in our lives. We all experience losing a loved one. We all experience disappointments of all different kinds. In these times, our closest ally is our honesty before God and before those closest to us. We need to just be who we are, feel what we need to feel, and accept the process during these days. When we do this, we can often see how those days are not only the kind of days that can turn to be a blessing, but they can also be the kind of days that bring us even closer to the divine calling and purpose that God has for us.

I personally had great struggle with stuttering when I was a very young. I remember having to fight and fight to make sure my words came out just the way I wanted. They didn't come out naturally. I remember that reading aloud was the thing I dreaded the most in school because I knew that I would have problems with my stutter, and I did. I still remember in the sixth grade I was called on to read, and I was so nervous that I stuttered throughout the enter time I was reading. After I finished, I hid my head behind the book in tears because I knew that everyone probably thought I was so stupid. When I was in college, I spent week after week after week reading aloud in front of my friends. By my third year of college, I was giving messages to my audiences, and now I speak publicly and get paid for it! Not only that, but I can now speak two languages fluently. When I look back, I smile at those days because God gave me double for every hard thing I went through! I am so thankful to God. And He's going to do that same in your life as well!

What I am saying is we do not have to let any day change who we know our God is. God is great and God is good. God makes quality days, and I like to say that we are all coming from a blessing, currently in a blessing, or running into a blessing! I am here to tell you that even those days that seem tough are still good, if not of even greater quality, because they are there to make you so much better than you could ever dream of or imagine, and plus God will not allow you to go through anything more than you can handle (see 1Corinthians 10:13).

Let's look at Jesus with His disciples. Jesus asked His disciples to cross over the Sea of Galilee knowing that there would be a storm coming up ahead. So why did Jesus allow them to go into this storm? In order to strengthen their faith in the One who sent them, and because He was the same One who told them, "We are going TO CROSS OVER to the other side." In all the places in the New Testament where the disciples face a storm, Jesus addresses their faith. I believe that there is something here for us to see. The storms of life are there to strengthen us. So here is the thing with Jesus, the storms of life won't stop you from getting to your destination, but rather it propels you to your destiny and propels you to be an even greater blessing. So declare that your day is either good quality or even greater quality, especially when the days seem to not have high quality at all. Best believe that each day is very high quality and God is propelling you to greater things.

From High Quality Day to High Quality Person

I need to be the first person to admit that I used to be all about chasing after those high quality days. I would get so upset with people if they seemed to even slightly ruin the potential of my high quality day. I was trying to take control of those around me because I was so afraid of ruining my perfect day! Now, I understand that this is a bit of nonsense. I now try to focus more on being a quality person. I try to focus on how God is more interested in improving the quality of my character than He is with improving the quality of my day.

So how can we grow day by day as a high quality person? Start from the inside. Start to understand deeply how you are a high quality person. Know that God is good and that He has the greatest of good in store for you. The Bible says, *"No eye has seen, no ear has heard, no heart has fully imagined what good God has in store for His people"* (1 Corinthians 2:9). You were made wonderfully by God. You are His spectacular handiwork, His workmanship, His beautiful creation (see Ephesians 2:10)! I encourage you to say these things repeatedly in the mirror or on your way home or to work. Let it sink deeply down inside you. You are wonderfully made by God. You are His marvelous masterpiece.

Also, understand how God wants to bring some amazing good into your life right now. God is good, but here is the thing I want to challenge you with: practice thinking of the highest, most spectacular good you could ever think of or imagine for a person and don't hold back! Perhaps think of your best friend, or maybe a family member you love, or someone else in your family (that maybe you don't quite love as much). Now, think of what you want for that person and the highest, most greatest good that we could ever think of or imagine for that person. This doesn't even match to a drop of water in the ocean to what God has for us. Do you believe it?

Do not limit God. I want you to know that your dreams from God include all that, but so much more! We think that since the Bible says, "my ways are not your ways" that God doesn't want to give us the things that we consider to be good things. Wrong! Why wouldn't God want your friends to be set free? Why wouldn't God want to restore what the enemy took from them? He placed our dreams in our hearts in the first place.

Don't be a bully!

Let's talk prosperity for a moment. I am fully aware of the idea of prosperity out there, especially in the Christian world. I'm not talking in this book about prosperity in the way that it is conveyed through the media these days, but I also don't want to steer away from it either because God makes it clear that He wants all His people to be blessed and to be a blessing. I have to admit, I was also a prosperity-police-Christian. I would look at people and make sure that when they ask for that new car that they really needed it! I would ask others, "Now, do you really need this or that?" I started to discover that not only was I ineffective in changing their desires, but they also stopped sharing things with me. You might say, "Good, you don't need to hear from a selfish person like that anyway!" But here's the problem — I also have desires that someone else might think are too much or too little. Am I supposed to gauge the value of my desires based off of what others think about them? And, how does Joe or Sarah know that what I am asking is out of need or not? I believe that these days when we talk about prosperity with each other, we have started eating each other alive, and we bully each other until we stop sharing what we desire at all, which can be depressing.

Let's Be Honest...

I confess that I was a prosperity bully, too, and tried to force people to "think like a Christian." I didn't desire prosperity for their lives until I learned that this was really my pride and self-centeredness which said, "I know what God wants for everybody." And even worse, I would say to myself, "Jeremy, lay low, don't do too much, don't do too little, just be in-between, or God will get you!" Instead, I decided to learn how to just be honest with God. I encourage you to do the same and just be honest with God about everything in your life.

Now I know some have said, "What about the guy in the Bible that said, 'Don't give me too much, don't give me too little, just give me my daily bread?'" Yes, this man is a great example. This man is an example to us that we need to understand what we can handle. We are not to be ashamed if we have too much or too little. And yet we are so quick to condemn those who have "too much," and this is just as wrong as ripping on those who have "too little." For fun, let's compare this man with Jabez in the Bible. What is the difference between the man asking for just his daily bread, and Jabez who asked to be blessed indeed? They both knew what they wanted and asked God for it. They both knew they could ask and receive from God. They both wanted to please God with what they had.

I can't tell you what to ask God for, but I can tell you that whatever you have is meant to be pleasing to Him. I can tell you that God loves you and is pleased with you. I can tell you that you can be open and honest with God. He is not here to condemn you for having too much or too little. God has everything! So just be honest with God.

What do you want?

Also, it doesn't hurt to know what you want out of life. If you want to be blessed indeed like Jabez, then pray it! If you want to only have your daily bread like the man in Proverbs 30, then pray that, but know what you want! I have seen people who sit back and criticize others for having too much or too little. Look, I believe this is an action that doesn't please God. You decide what you want, and the rest is up to God. Jesus asked the blind men, "What do you want Me to do for you?" Jesus is asking you this now.

What do you want God to do for you in your life? Not like a genie, but like a good Father. Tell the Father, tell

YOUR Father, what you want, and don't be ashamed. In other words, talk to Him… Don't be afraid to let Him know your hurts, your pains, your thoughts, and the things you desire. Again, whatever you do, don't be ashamed to lay all your cares before God. So many Christians fall for this trap— they bully themselves into not wanting to look selfish, so they don't share with God what they want. I believe that this is so backwards because what ends up happening is, O yes, they learn how to look holy, but the truth is that they stopped talking to God altogether because they feel too ashamed to speak to Him about anything. They think He might condemn them and say, "Why are you asking me these things!? You are so self-absorbed and stubborn! What is your problem!?" We think God will step away from us if we are honest with Him, but I am saying here that it is just the opposite. Share with Him EVERYTHING. That's how we normally define a healthy relationship.

So, can I tell you that if you want…dare I say… a CAR, ask God and then repent for being such a heathen! Just kidding. But if you want a warm place to stay, then that is what you want! No hiding or pretending. It is what it is! Stop judging yourself and just be yourself with God. God is big enough and can handle you and all your craziness. Let Him determine what you really need in your life. Your job is to just ask and then trust. He loves you too much to give you ten cars just because you asked for it, or He may give you two cars because He wants you to give one to a loved one. God does what He wants. Be open with God. Be honest with Him. He knows what's best for you. Don't hold back from Him, and He will not hold back from you. God says, *"Return to me, and I will return to you"* Zechariah 1:3. I encourage you to just tell God what you want and have an open and honest relationship with Him today.

Epiphany #8: God made Goodness

Let me tell you something: God made goodness. We all know what goodness is, but sometime we are afraid to imagine or think of what is good in our lives for many reasons. I want to challenge you. We've known what is good from back when we were born; all those things that make us genuinely smile are good things. Now start to imagine! God wants us to genuinely smile, and smile EVERY DAY. He's given us EVERYTHING. It is up to us to receive them by faith today.

Repetition is good so I will mention it again. God is good, y'all! Think of the good we know of and let me tell you, it's only so far greater, so much greater in the heart of our God! It may be unimaginable at times, but I want you to know that the feelings you feel when you experience the most good life is a drop in the bucket in comparison to how much good God wants to bring into your life. It is all that, and then so much more! "All that" is to say this: Experience God, and you will find out for yourself that you can trust God, that you can be happy in Him, that you can rest in Him; He can give you peace, He can give you joy, He can arrest your worry, He can bring you to life again, He can restore your soul, He can refresh your spirit, He can give you great contentment, right now. I repeat: This is the day the Lord has made. Let us be full of joy and be glad in it!

Epiphany #9: Give to God your Tuesday in the Highest!

I've gone through many days just coasting by, and often I find that the day didn't go as well as I wanted. Tuesdays just seemed to be one of those blah days to me. It's like one of the least expected days that I would see God move. This mundaneness happened whenever I didn't prescribe to the day what it needed with my words. So how do we do that?

Pretend today is Tuesday. The word of God says, "Glory to God in the highest!" I heard a song that sung, "In the Highest", and I just kept thinking about that title. And I thought to myself, "What does 'In the Highest' mean?" I concluded that it is praising God with the greatest of joy, the greatest of an excited heart and attitude—especially the kind that doesn't depend on external circumstances. God wants us to decide to worship Him. Our decision to worship Him no matter what, is giving "praise to God in the Highest!"

So for no other reason except to the One who matters most: God deserves the highest praise! I dare you to stop whatever you're doing right now and just give to God your Tuesday in the Highest! You may lift your hands or use your voice, but I encourage you to not to let this day pass without giving this to God. Give to God your work in the Highest! Give to God your heart in the Highest! If you see something encouraging, share it. I see people all around the world worshiping the King—Jesus who is King of All kings and Lord of All lords. Name above all names! Jesus! We give to you, Oh God, Our Tuesday in the Highest!

Wow, now I'm getting excited just writing this! For all of us, especially those who are "dignified," a little praise break might be just what we need to bring some life into our lives. This isn't just an excitement thing. This is a new movement, a great moving. Your Tuesdays will never be the same again; I speak a powerful Tuesday from now on in your life. In Jesus' name, Amen.

Chapter Four

A Complete 180 Degree Smile

Epiphany #10. Looking on the big, BIG sacrifices of others with gratitude. Jesus died to put a smile on your and my face.

This is the meat of the entire book! So now, I will brave you!

Don't you dare live one moment in sorrow. Blood was shed for you to enjoy. Now, let me stop and tell you that many individuals, especially in the United States where I am from, experience depression because they feel pressure to perform based on what this world tells them, and not on what God has placed in their hearts. Their existence feels threatened every day by a world that yells distractions at them! But God tells us, *"Greater is He that is within you than he that is within the world" (1 John 4:4).*

That's so right! Hear that voice inside saying, "Enjoy your life to the fullest!" That is God's end desire for His servants (See Matthew 25:23), to His own Glory. God - Jesus - died on a cross so that He could put a smile on your face. God wants you to smile forever! If you're going to have an eternal smile, you need to surrender your life to God today. Give Him your life. He promises joy, peace, and complete enjoyment of your life. No, not a Rolls Royce, a platinum watch, a whatever-karat gold watch, but joy, peace, and complete enjoyment of your life, which is far greater than anything you can buy on earth. On the flip side, I know preachers these days say, "Oh no, when you give your life to Christ, everything's not peachy keen, in fact things can be so horrible gloomy and sad, so don't expect bubbly glitter feelings." WRONG! Pastors that say that don't understand that Apostle Paul shared those things that he suffered as the torrents that bring even greater and unexplainable joy!

So I'm saying EXPECT IT! Expect the joy that overtakes the world! Expect a song that will shake the foundations of this world! Expect a laugh that will make the enemy weep in silence! Expect a song that will unite and encourage a nation of one! Expect it! Smile! You have full permission to smile! Take on Christ. His yoke is easy, and His burden is light. His blood was shed for you to put a smile on your face, have glittery feelings, and DON'T YOU DARE hold back! Don't you dare feel bad about it! Jesus died for you! And behold, HE IS RISEN! So now BE BOLD and smile! Now, don't you dare stop rejoicing!!! Let's say it again, CHRIST IS RISEN! Amen!

Epiphany #11: Repentance for many of us can now have a new meaning: EXPRESSING JOY!

Repentance for most of us is a bad thing. But what has happened of recent days is that a wrong picture of repentance has been around giving us the wrong ideas about it. We think that repentance means we are supposed to be gloomy all of the time. We think, therefore, it is our job to show people how sad and serious we are, and then people will come to know about grace, joy, and abundant life of Jesus. That, my friends, is an idea going in the wrong direction. And so repentance is a complete 180 degrees from that kind of life.

I bet you know some people that ought to change their mourning into dancing, change their frowns into smiles, trade their tears of sadness into tears of uncontrollable joy! Repentance for many of us will mean to smile and to accept others in our lives. Repentance might mean to express joy and love in our lives from our hearts, and make it a new habit to do so.

Life in Christ is not meant to be a sad, condemning lifestyle, but rather it is a joyful, happy and giving lifestyle because of the power within you that gives you great amazing grace to overcome all things! Even at times where it seems we should be the other way, it's the power of Jesus Christ who we turn to that gives us power to overcome and rejoice in times of trouble; we praise, and God gives us unexplainable joy, and that joy comes from Jesus and turns into power, and that power motivates us to love. (check out Psalm 23, Ephesians 3:23, and 2 Chronicles 2:17. These are great examples.)

Remember, if you are NOT where you want to be in your life, repent, and God PROMISES that He will take you not only to where you want to be, but He promises over and over beyond your wildest dreams, far beyond where you ever dreamed you would be. Because, although we may think we want something superficially, what we really long for only comes through praise and worshiping God. Praise Him, AND GUESS WHAT?? YOU ARE ALREADY THERE!

So die to dead and dreary ideas, then you can say...

Epiphany #12: I DIE DAILY

What does the phrase "I die daily" mean? In 1 Corinthians 15:31, the Apostle Paul says, "I die daily", speaking about the dangers he faces due to the hope he professed in the resurrection of Jesus Christ. Today, Christians use the term, "I die daily" as a way of saying "I sacrifice my lifestyle of pursuing the pleasures of this world daily in order to pursue God." Yet, today it appears that many often take this to a legalistic level, to which the new pleasure is to avoid anything that has an appearance of joy or enjoyment in life, such as going to a movie or avoid taking your spouse or family on a vacation in order to look "holy". The phrase "I die daily" used to mean to me, "I do things I hate doing," or "I do many works to prove myself a good person," but now I know it means to give God praise. Honor Him with worship. Say, "Thank You" to Him for who He is.

"Thank you" is the door we open to a room of praise and worship. "I die to myself" means doing what it takes to give praise to God and stay in that place of thanksgiving. Let's look at David.

David could not praise and honor God by sitting down. He had to dance! Now that was a great example of an "I die daily" mentality. Dying daily is giving glory, not to ourselves, but to God, and God requires the praises of His people! We praise Him to give him the highest honor! We die because the alternative to praising God is praising ourselves and we think by doing all this extra hard work that God is somehow pleased at our self-sacrifice. But it is when we express joy and delight in Him at work or at home that God smiles and we die to our own praise (and, for that matter, to any other thing).

So only to Him, and with a great big smile, we praise because God has truly been good to us! Praise Him! Praise Him with the lyre! Praise Him with the trumpet (see Psalm 150)! As they used to say in the old gospel church, "Praise Him! Praise Him! Praise Him in the morning! Praise Him in the noon day! Praise Him! Praise Him! Praise Him when the sun goes down!" Amen.

Chapter Five

Where to Find Your Smile

Epiphany #13: All of your dreams are waiting for you in a land called obedience.

There are dreams and prayers I'm sure we all have. Sometimes we wonder why some of our dreams and desires fulfilled seem to be held from us. Well, after a while it came to my attention that our prayers may not be held from us more than they are waiting for us. There is a land called "Obedience," and as long as you stay in another area, they (our answered prayers) won't be seen. My suggestion for myself and anyone else is: Walk towards "Obedience" today. How? Be honest to God. Be very open and very honest to God who *is* love (see 1 John 4:8).

He who was open and honest to you first. Jesus revealed God's honesty to us through His life and on the cross of Calvary. The road to the land of obedience is called "Open" and "Honest." Acknowledge God for who He really is: The Sovereign Ruler of all. Remember the story Jesus told of the man who wouldn't even so much as to look up to heaven, but rather beat his chest saying, "Have mercy on me, Lord, a sinner"? (see Luke 18:13). When you are open and honest with God, He will guide you. His Word reads: *"Do not have anxiety about anything, but in everything, by prayer and petition, with giving thanks, make your wants known to God. And the peace of God which transcends all understanding with protect your hearts and your minds and guide you in Christ Jesus"* (See Philippians 4:6, 7).

Praying that all your dreams come true in the place of Obedience today. There is no safer place to be than in the place of obedience because God promises you'll have the peace of God to take you wherever you go. Obedience can turn your dry city into a metropolis. In fact, I would dare to say that is the plan God has for you, being in that place you are right now. Don't see this so much as a physical metropolis, but rather a spiritual one. God wants to make you a metropolis from the inside out. He wants to turn your soul into a metropolis for people to see God and be greatly refreshed. Thank Him and watch Him transform your life.

Epiphany #14: The decision to abound! Here is the key and here is the goal—Abounding in thanksgiving

Easy abounding

If there was another place where you could find your smile, the place would be called "gratitude" or "thanksgiving." So how do we *abound* in thanksgiving?

First, I'm not going to lie to you: this IS going to be easy. Easier than you think. I say this not only because all of books tell you that "this is not going to be easy!" but because I want you to get into the mind frame of God; in other words, we are used to thinking, "this is going to be so hard," but God never thinks that way. His angels know this. That's why the angel told the servant of the Lord, "Nothing is too hard for God."

So I tell you that thinking authentically positive about your life is a very simple and easy thing for you, if you dare to do it, and the Holy Spirit's work inside of you is also done easily with grace. Pray for the Holy Spirit's help, *"And God is able to make all grace abound to you, so that always having all sufficiency in everything, you may have an abundance for every good deed" (2 Corinthians 9:8).*

Abounding in thanksgiving

"Therefore, as you received Christ Jesus the Lord, so walk in him, rooted and built up in him and established in the faith, just as you were taught, abounding in thanksgiving" (Colossians 2:6-7). So, how do we abound with thanksgiving? It's a habit. These are non-negotiable. Visualize the consequences. I say to myself: On the law of the lord I meditate both day and night (See Psalm 1:2). I will therefore keep my mind stayed on Christ (See Isaiah 26:3). I will fix my eyes on Jesus (See Hebrews 12:2).

We tend to take seriously the things we perceive as reality in our lives. The Word of God is in fact the reality that is keeping this world with good still in it. The world and the devil have lied to us, telling us, "Oh, you can't keep your mind on Christ at ALL times!" Do not believe that. Remember, if the Bible said it, you, yes even you, can do it! Therefore, we must pay attention to what we are saying to ourselves.

Epiphany #15: Talk more to yourself. Tell yourself to smile.

We've heard it said, "Don't talk to yourself." But this is a terrible lie because the truth is that we talk to ourselves in our minds all the time. Can you imagine living with someone and telling yourself that you are not supposed to talk to that person your whole life? The truth is that we talk to ourselves all the time, and we are either saying to ourselves, "You can do it!" or "You cannot do it!" David, speaking to his very soul, said, *"Praise the Lord, my soul; all my inmost being, praise his holy name. Praise the Lord, my soul, and forget not all his benefits"(Psalm 103:1-2).* David spoke to himself all the time, and told himself to turn his attention towards the Lord. Let's do the same.

Epiphany #16: Keep your mind stayed on Christ

I personally like to have certain things in the house to stay there all the time. I love it when I find the perfect outlet in the house for me to put my computer and other tech stuff. When I find a place that is good for something, I love it to simply stay there. I think when it comes to our thoughts, it's best for us when our minds stay on things that really matter.

Isaiah says, *"You will keep in perfect peace those whose minds are steadfast, because they trust in you" (Isaiah 26:3).* Another translation says, "whose minds are *stayed* on Thee" (KJV). Many of us are tempted to not take this very seriously. We might say that we cannot keep our minds stayed on Christ all the time, and so we are defeated even before we try. Now, I'm telling you, it's a simple thing, but it's up to you to DECIDE to keep your mind stayed on Christ. And it's up to you to allow your mind to be stayed on noble things. I encourage you not to accept anything less. You were made to keep your mind stayed on the things of Christ.

> *"Finally, brethren, whatever is true, whatever is honorable, whatever is right, whatever is pure, whatever is lovely, whatever is of good repute, if there is any excellence and if anything worthy of praise, let your mind dwell on these things" (Philippians 4:8).*

"Dwell on these things" means just that—think on these things—meditate upon them, revolve them in your minds, seriously consider them, and reason with yourselves about them, in order to put them into practice. Now if you believed that you couldn't do this, then you would never start. Decide not to fall for this. Decide not to pay attention to anything other than what is noble, pure, and good for one year and see how your life will change. And if it's hard, for goodness sake, don't just accept that it is hard. Have you ever played pretend when you were little? Well, pretend it's easy and you will find that it is easier than you think. Yes, I say pretend because we usually just don't give ourselves permission to be creative, and to put it plainly, we can often times be our worst enemy. So just pretend you are who God calls you to be, and besides, God's word says you are and you can. So who are you to question that? "Believe" is the first step towards the goal. *For as he thinketh in his heart, so is he (Proverbs 23:7 NKJ).*

Let's see this verse again: *"And God is able to bless you abundantly, so that in all things at all times, having all that you need, you will abound in every good work" (2 Corinthians 9:8).*

Let's look more into what it means to abound in thanksgiving. If it's there, it will show. For example, financially, if someone is abounding in their finances, typically even if they try to hide it, it eventually becomes obvious; it is evident in one way or another that this person has wealth. Perhaps it is reflected in the way the person is living or in what the person has. In any case, it's there.

In the same way, abounding in thanksgiving means that it is as if a person is wearing thanksgiving all over and it couldn't be hidden if they tried! Thanksgiving can't be hidden; it would be like wearing a bright colored shirt that is so radiant everybody can see! That's what I want! I want to wear thanksgiving brightly to the point that it's evident for everyone, so that everyone can benefit from and latch on to it! I want to have that kind of radiance! This doesn't have to only come from money. This can also come from a heart of gratitude.

When I walk these days, I think of others and what they've done to help me. I remembered while teaching English in South Korea, a brother who told me I came to his mind gave me two shirts that his family sent to him from Philadelphia. I remembered to thank my friend Mike who took a video of me as I sang a song of encouragement for a friend in a café (thanks Mike!). I remembered to thank all those who listened to my songs and gave me encouragement, "liking" my songs on Facebook. I knew that what they did made me feel good, but I'm so thankful to

God that it came to my mind and I said, "Oh, I should thank them for that!" What has someone done for you, and have you stopped just to message a quick, "thank you for that btw*." Do that right now.

Here is a definition I found for abounding: To have in large number or amounts of something. Another way to define abounding is: more than enough. Perhaps abounding means that you grow a "thankful muscle" and build a habit for life that your children's children can carry with them. Today I am thankful for you and I'm cheering you on!

Start in small steps today. Think of three things you are thankful for. For those of you who want to start by sprinting, I'm not a fan of competition, but I think this would be a worthy competition to see how many ways can you think of the persons in your day to day life, at home, at work, and out passing by, how many items of thanks can you give for each person. Thank you, Lord, for such amazing goodness that surrounds us every day. I dare to look around me and see Your awesomeness and Your great goodness! Awaken my heart, mind, and soul to Your goodness today.

"Therefore, as you received Christ Jesus the Lord, so walk in him, rooted and built up in him and established in the faith, just as you were taught, ABOUNDING IN THANKSGIVING" (Colossians 2:6-7, emphasis mine).

*by the way

Chapter Six

Put a Smile in your Routine

Epiphany #17: Clothes from God

Today, my 11-month-old daughter was making her usual very cute noises after she woke up. We went to her room to see her. Our little girl is growing up. Soon she'll be putting on her own socks and shoes. That to me is just a mind blowing concept right now! But eventually, it's going to happen. So what about you? You've learned how to put on the right clothing before leaving to go school or to go work, but have you learned how to put on love in the morning?

Our spiritual body is much like the physical in that it needs daily attending to. Today, I challenge you to put on these spiritual qualities. Start with love. I start with reading the Bible and getting my mind focused on what the day is all about. Today I read about how the people of God are blessed and cannot in any way be cursed. How about starting the day like that!

Every second of every day is a chance to put on Love. It is the most meaningful gift we can, and will, ever have. It will be the most meaningful gift we can and will ever give. What do we do with every moment? We put on love. Now think of this: do we have to keeping putting on clothes every moment of every day? That's a silly idea! We put our clothes on in the morning. It's one of the first things we do, and it's a non-negotiable for many reasons. In Northwest Ohio, it gets pretty cold in the winter time. I need some extra layers of clothing sometimes, depending on the weather. It's the same spiritually. Before the hustle and bustle, before the spiritual weather gusts, we need to be clothed. Colossians 3:14 reads, *"Above all these put on love, which binds everything together in perfect harmony."* When we put on love in the morning, just like clothing, we might have to put on some more layers during the day, but I like it because prophecies pronounced after the incident are not as effective. You need to pronounce that, "This is the day the LORD has made and I WILL rejoice and be glad in it" before the day's events accrue. Every moment of the day is a gift, and the way we start and finish the day can make an extremely big difference on how the middle will go.

Last night, I made a list before I went to bed of the things I would do the next day. I do this because I don't want to wonder what my day will be like when I wake up in the morning. I want to be ahead of the game and pray for my rest, and my family's day tomorrow. Then, when I get up in the morning I can pray and not be distracted by wondering what the day will bring. Some of my friends, like me, plan out the week before the week starts. My wife and I manage our money for the month. We desire to manage the money for every month before the month starts, so that we have a head start and vision for the month. Why don't you set out to see how much thanksgiving and love you'd determine to have in your life by next week, month, etc.? In a moment, I will give a practical way this can be done.

Jesus prayed in the morning and set the course for putting on love every moment of everyday of His life. We see now that every moment of Jesus' life was held and captured into purpose! Look back at Jesus' life while He was here over 2,000 years ago. Every moment was surrendered to the will of God. Every moment of His life was filled with the power of God's love, and so can that be for us and for everyone who belongs to Jesus. In Christ, there is no moment in your life that is meaningless or without purpose. It's all there with the opportunity for us to put on love and see God's powerful work in our lives. I pray that His love changes me and you, and today we see change in our lives and in the lives of those around us as we hold every moment as an opportunity to humbly put on the love of Jesus.

A way that you could do this is by planning on your calendar. Recently, my wife and I decided to start our planning on the calendar in the same order that we place our priorities. We start by setting on our calendar two-weeks ahead, the things related to our relationship to God, and place them on our calendar. Then we go to what things we want to do to enrich our marriage and place those on the calendar, then family activities, and then friends/extended family, and finally career related. It is a constant reminder to us to remember to put on love and the things of God first in our lives before filling up our schedules with busy work. What are some other ways we can put on love and thanksgiving? Let's remember to put on love and thanksgiving today and intentionally place them on our calendars.

Epiphany #18: Give to God Your Best!

Okay, now that you're clothed, you're ready to go out and give to God your best. Think of these words in three parts:

1. "Give"
2. "To God"
3. "Your Best"

First, give.

God so loved the world that He gave. It is said that one of the greatest, if not the greatest sign of love is to give. In that case, what then can we give to God today? Let's think about this - how we can give it to God? Often, when we think of how we can give something to someone, we mistakenly think of how we would want to give it instead of how the receiver would like us to give. So let's think about this. How would God want us to give to Him? Let's see 2 Corinthians 9:7, "Each one must give as he has decided in his heart, not reluctantly or under compulsion, for God loves a cheerful giver." God loves it when we give with joy. With a genuine smile, knowing that God loves a cheerful giver and there isn't a way we can out give God because God loves these uber-givers so much that He'll give to the one who gives more to see him or her give and give again. Again, what can we give to God today? Let's do that with a smile and see God smile, too.

Second, to God.

When we give, two things to watch out for can often take place. We can either give for the wrong reasons, or we can simply lose sight of the reasons why we give in the first place. The reason is because it is "to God" that we give. For example, we often lose our patience with people and do not want to give to them our patience because we can easily forget that we are not giving ultimately to them, but to God. Whether we eat or we drink, or whatever we do, the most blessed thing is to let it be "To God" (see 1 Corinthians 10:31). This is important because it helps us to keep centered on why we do what we do, and we can grow less and less easily distracted by other motives because we stay centered on the reason why we give. It is to God.

As I write this book, on the days when I could easily write off (no pun intended) this book completely because I want to do other fun things, I am reminded that it is to God that I live, and it is to God that I am writing this book. This makes me greatly encouraged to write it and pray to God to bless the hands of every person who reads it. So, we remember that in all that we do and in all that we give, it is to God.

Third, our best.

A brief physics review. Don't worry, won't be on this topic too long if you don't like physics! The theory is that when energy is given, there is an equal return amount of work that must be equal to that energy. Hope I didn't lose everyone there! Anyway, so naturally, when we think of our best, we often think of becoming like Arnold Schwarzenegger in whatever field we are in. We think we need to be big, tough, and strong to be the best or to give our best. This could be. But I think it may help to think of our very best as not just effort, work and force, like with the most strongest person you can be, but instead as the most "you" that you can be; be the most authentic you. Now, I do not mean the "you" as in self-centered and self-focused person. I am fully aware that John the Baptist said, "I must decrease and He must increase." That doesn't mean that we need to pretend that John the Baptist didn't exist. Rather, it means that God needs to get the glory more and more out of our lives. Be the most authentic Sarah, James, or Tom that you can be, as in, be the person that God created you to be for His glory. This is important to realize because it may not look like anyone else's life, but it will glorify God most High. How do we know that giving our best is learning how to be our best us, so to speak? Because in order to be your best "you", you need to find out who you really are, and that requires having a dear and close relationship with Him who created you. The best "you" can only come out of Him. The best way that you can be and give your best is by first getting to know the One who created you and talking with Him throughout each day. That is how you and I become the most that God created us to be, and to give to God our best.

David used a sling and a stone, with no armor to defeat Goliath – a very unlikely strategy to destroy a giant who was many feet taller than you and I! But David defeated him swiftly because he was aware of who God made him to be, and therefore it was unfathomable being anything or anyone else. He learned this by simply spending time with God. And we are all God's workmanship, His wonderful handiwork and His masterpiece (Ephesians 2:10), so wouldn't it be rather frustrating if you made and a hammer that keeps trying to be a nail? No, let's flow into the person God made us to be.

We will talk about King David again later in this chapter. But the best way you can give to God your best is to start by knowing who we are as a child of God. You are a child of the Most High God. Walk and talk in that revelation, that you are a child of the King. You are His child, a child of the King of Kings and Lord of Lords! The Maker of Heaven and Earth made you for His great awesome and specific purpose. To be His own. Meditate on that for a while and giving-to-God-your-best will be something that happens as a bi-product.

Think about your unique talents, and offer them to this world. Our unique talents are here to bring change, and even healing, to this world. They are here for no other reason!

Do not worry about the things that you think are against you. It's those very things that God wants to turn into a symbol of victory for you in your life! Think about the cross.

There was a time when the cross was the most disliked message in the world. And today it expresses the most beautiful love man has and will ever know on this earth. The cross is a testimony to the victory over sin forever! It is a symbol of what every Christian is supposed to be in Jesus.

What are our lives here for? What are we here for? Go ahead and ask yourself this question. I declare that we are here to see God turn the most horrible things in this world into transformed, incredible, and beautiful creations once and for all to God's glory!

You are a ground breaker! You are salt to this world (see Matthew 5:13). You are a great flavor to this world. You are a life preserver. You bring much flavor to life! Salt up this world. Be bold. Be brave! Bring newness that changes this world. Keep disclosing what God has always been putting in your heart: to change this world for the good that He prepared for you to do before the creation of this world. Be bold. Be humble. Use your talents and don't be ashamed to use them. Pray for opportunities to use them and make the very best of them!

I don't care what anyone says, numbers matter. You are a number. You are numbered with the saints, so remember that. You count! When you go to a room don't back down because you're in a room of 10, 20, or 2000. Use your gifts to the fullest. They are God's gifts to you. In fact, they are what people need in this world. Let's give to God - now - our best! This is the 24-hour period in which you will have a tremendous day!

I'd like to drive this point home for you. Giving to God our best is closely related to harnessing the power and influence of our God-given strengths and talents in our lives, so it is important to pray and discover what they are. As you focus on harnessing your talents to help others, take some time, pray and ask God about how you can give to God all your very best talents today! Remember that your best doesn't, and will not necessarily look, exactly like the best of someone else. We all have been given very specific talents (see Romans 12:4-8). We must stop to understand who God has made us to be, and then rest in the peace of how God wants us to give Him our very best. Another way to say "focus on your talents" is to focus on the things you *can* do very well that uplifts others, and do that. The gifts and talents that we have are in close relationship with the callings we have been given. Spend less time on the things you realize are not closely related to your calling, and more time on the things that are. For me, I am challenging myself to give my best passion and my heart to God when I lead worship. I am certainly a fan of focusing on my strengths and making sure that they give the fullest glory to God! Sometimes, we think that giving our best to God means to start thinking of our weaknesses and all the problems we have, and then try to fix only those. Now, of course, if we are doing something that is displeasing to God and we want to get right with God, by all means we are to take it seriously and get unnecessary distractions out of our lives so we can focus more on a healthy relationship with God and others. My point is we are not to compare our talents with anyone else's, and therefore try to improve on a skill set that we were never meant to have! We have to understand that we are to use what we have right now, and that God has the power to multiply what we have! Often times, we think that we need to make a specific quality better, but if a comedian thought he needed to be less spontaneous and more serious, he may accomplish his goal, but he may also lose the impact that he might have had on his purpose to make other people laugh! I would challenge you to do an inventory of your own gifts and start polishing and building on your God-given gifts and talents so that you can be fully equipped for God's specific purpose for your life. For everything else, pray and get the support that you need from people who have other talents. We all need each other. Find the assistance you need so that your weaknesses aren't in the way, but never try to focus solely on improving your weaknesses. Manage your weaknesses, but harness the power and influence of your God-given strengths and talents. God promises that He will take care of the rest.

"Each of you should use whatever gift you have received to serve others, as faithful stewards of God's grace in its various forms. If anyone speaks, they should do so as one who speaks the very words of God. If anyone serves, they should do so with the strength God provides, so that in all things God may be praised through Jesus Christ. To him be the glory and the power for ever and ever. Amen" (1 Peter 4:10-11 NIV).

Chapter Seven

Smiling When It's Hard to...

Epiphany #19: How can our conflicts put a smile on our face?

We've been talking a great deal about the good. So what about the bad and the ugly? Well, often times (in fact, I would say every time) when we have conflicts, it's important to note that usually our conflicts have nothing to do with the person we are in conflict with, but everything to do with us: the development of our own character and what God is trying to do in and through you and me to change us and to grow us.

Check out Genesis 9:20-23: *"Noah, a man of the soil, proceeded to plant a vineyard. When he drank some of its wine, he became drunk and lay uncovered inside his tent. Ham, the father of*

Canaan, saw his father naked and told his two brothers outside. But Shem and Japheth took a garment and laid it across their shoulders; then they walked in backward and covered their father's naked body. Their faces were turned the other way so that they would not see their father naked."

What was Ham's mistake? He told on his father to his brothers. It seems innocent, but God didn't think so. Often times we learn about the sins of others, and whether it's voluntarily or involuntarily, the question isn't what the person did, but rather how we responded with what we heard or saw. That will determine and reflect what kind of person we are and will become.

Ham was not wise in this way. Ham didn't realize Noah had authority from God to bless or curse Ham's future. He did not regard authority and order in this way. He did not think much of how he conducted himself. Let me stop here to say "ignorance is bliss" is not good when it comes to knowing our ways. The Bible says we are to ask God to search our hearts so that we may turn and pursue His ways (see Psalm 139:23). In Ham telling his brothers, he was actually hurting himself. Love does not expose sin to others, but covers and protects at all times.

On the other hand, Ham's brothers took action in that they covered their father's shortcomings. They refused even the knowledge of knowing their father's shortcoming and shame. When Shem and Japheth heard from their brother, they didn't scold Ham. They immediately took extra effort to take a garment and lay it across their shoulders, and then they laid the garment over their father. Walking backwards, their faces were turned the other way so that they would not even see their father's nakedness. Now, which is easier to do: tell others, or walk backwards, covering, looking the other way? Obviously the second is harder to do. So why did they do it? For honor. They knew that they needed to honor their father. This is so beautiful. The brothers took the extra effort to ignore their father's shortcomings. Now, of course, they did not completely ignore their father's shortcomings, but they did something in love and honor to cover him. I believe that this is something almost completely lost in a culture that jumps on every opportunity to "help" others by pointing out their flaws. We can learn a lot from these two brothers. Shem and Japheth, never tried to change Noah. They never pulled Noah over and had an intervention with him. I am not saying that interventions are bad, and I think there is a time to confront someone for sure, but the point is that these brothers only focused on loving and honoring their father, and according to the passage, that was the only thing that counted. Have we done this in our lives? Have we taken the time to cover our friends and family with love?

Let's think about it in another way: Nowadays we need to be careful about the things we see on television and other places when we go out and about. Eighty percent or more of the time on television, we are just watching different people have Noah-moments, and we need to learn to cover them, and simply not look at them, but instead put a veil over the television and get to our own work.

Epiphany #20: Cover them

Honor doesn't take many words or thoughts, but much prayer and much action in love. Let me say it again: honoring others takes prayer and action, not as much thoughts and words. We don't need to spend much time in conversation or thought about the situation when it comes to conflicts. The world needs action in love. I'm not saying that conversation is not useful, but when the focus is only on the

know the commandments: 'You shall not murder, you shall not commit adultery, you shall not steal, you shall not give false testimony, you shall not defraud, honor your father and mother.'" Then the man said, "All things I kept since I was a boy." The Bible says that at this very moment *Jesus looked at him and loved him.* Then Jesus said, "Go, sell everything you have and give to the poor, and you will have treasure in heaven. Then come, follow me." And at this, the man fell face down to the ground and he was very sad because he was really rich. Jesus then turned to his disciples and told them how hard it is for people who depend on their stuff to be able God's kingdom, yet he said, "With man this is impossible, but not with God; all things are possible with God!"

Earlier I mentioned that we were made to make people smile, but that does not mean that we were made to please people all the time. It means something different altogether. Did you catch the part during the conversation between the rich man and Jesus when, after the man said that he kept all of the commandments, the Bible says that "at this Jesus looked at him and loved him." Real love is going to cause us to put our smiles on reserve in order to bring a bigger smile later. At the end of this account all we see is a man walking away. We don't know if after this the same man came back to the disciples and didn't give everything he had and lived a very blessed and rich life both inside and out! Jesus told this man the truth so that he could later receive something much greater than physical wealth and riches.

Sometimes we will have to do this as well. We will have to be bold and brave enough to care love and tell people the truth, again with great love. I am becoming more and more convinced that truth ought never to be present without love right there by its side. If we are bold enough to tell the truth, then we ought to be brave enough to carry it with love. If you aren't willing to love the person when you speak to them, consider staying silent until you are able. Consider not letting any unwholesome talk come out of your mouth about them (see Ephesians 4:19). Only consider how you can help put a smile on their face. Let them know how much you care about them, and I promise you that they will not be able to justify their frown for long if what you have done was in truth genuine and authentic love. Try it today. Love others with your God given truth today.

Choosing to smile

When all is said and done, if you can't find any external reason to smile, you can smile at the fact that you can still choose to smile. You can still choose to smile in the days and years to come. You can smile because you have the privilege of making the decision to in midst of sorrow and suffering. In midst of it all, you can choose to smile because God gave you the precious gift of choice and no one will be able to take it away from you. In the Bible, Joshua, who led the people of Israel into their promised land, said to them after they settled, *"But if serving the Lord seems undesirable to you, then choose for yourselves this day whom you will serve, whether the gods your ancestors served beyond the Euphrates, or the gods of the Amorites, in whose land you are living. But as for me and my household, we will serve the Lord"* (Joshua 24:15).

At some point, we all have to simply choose to rejoice. Rejoicing and putting a smile on your face is a choice that we all can make. If we are honest, the truth is that we let external things cause us not to smile. In a sense, we give our smiles away to things that aren't worthy of affecting them. At the end of the day, it all comes down to whom or what we see is bigger than our problems. Are we focused heavily on the size of our own problems? Are we examining and trying to know the ins and outs of each part of our little world? Or are we examining the goodness and greatness, and the awesomeness of our God? As I have mentioned, there is always a time to mourn, and there is a time to have some sorrow. Weeping may endure for a night, but joy comes in the morning. And the favor of God very far outweighs the troubles (see Psalm 30:5). By the way - I know which one you are, or you wouldn't be reading this book!

After a close look at the size of our God, we can't help but to laugh at the face of our past and our future. God caused Joseph to simply forget his past because of God's goodness in his life! (see Genesis 41:51). The woman of noble character laughed and smiled at her future because of how awesome it was. Now it's your turn! Get around people now who see any problem the same way God does! Use a magnifying glass if you have to! Magnify every little blessing in your life. Your heart will fill up more and more. Today, see how God is bigger than your problems and see how He truly loves us and how He has so much; in fact, He has the best in store for each of us! Make magnifying the awesomeness of God in your life a simple habit.

If what I'm saying sounds strange, this being joyful about your life stuff may have to just be the "new normal" for you. If not for yourself, I would say this perspective is good to have just for the people around you whom you love. This is not being fake in my opinion, this is taking responsibility for your life and owning up to everything you've done and all the experiences you've had and simply say, "I'm not going to let these circumstances control my life anymore! I'm going to do something about this! Even if it kills me, I'm going to die pursuing the joy and peace the God promised to me! Because God wants me to smile I will choose to smile today!"

This is your time! You can choose to smile and free yourself from the chains that seem to have a hold on you. I can feel them slipping right now. For no reason at all, these chains are dropping and you are free and sound and whole in a way greater than ever before! God shines His light in your life today and you are completely whole, physically, spiritually, mentally, and emotionally! Let's just throw in financially as well! Because God wants you to be free from all things that enslaved you, you may not have dollars decreased from your debt today, but man and woman of

God, I pronounce that today is the beginning of a zero debt account in your bank account (legally and miraculously, of course)! Today is the day of new beginnings for you. You will smile more than you ever have, and it won't just be a fake smile! It will be a genuine smile and everyone will know that God put that smile on your face and they will rejoice! You will be a figure that will make many, I said many, people smile! Amen.

Epiphany #21: Godly interruptions (When things don't go as planned)

Conflicts usually result when things do not go as planned in our lives. But not every failed plan is bad. For example, I just had the best morning today with my wife. I know it sounds weird, but I confess that I only planned to have a *nice* morning, but not the best! We had the best breakfast and quiet time together. It was an overwhelming peaceful feeling just being there with good food and each other. We then turned and said to each other with a laugh, "This is how God interrupts our lives." It was an epiphany for me. God wants to give us a greater day. He wants to interrupt our lives with something more amazing than we could have ever planned.

He wants to detour your plans for the better. Are you up to it?

I want to encourage you to let God interrupt your day today with something greater. It was not expected, but I'd say this breakfast was one of the most joyous breakfast times we ever had. It wasn't just the food. It was the peace, the fact I had a day off, and our time in prayer before eating the breakfast at home. It was like everything was just another day, but when we prayed, God showed up! Again, God wants to interrupt your life today. Let Him surprise you with His goodness today. God is gracious and compassionate. He abounds in love (see Psalm 145:8). Show up, God! Show up in our lives today. Amen.

Chapter Eight

Envision your Smile

Epiphany #22: Visual map (Create a vision of people smiling)

So we have discussed how God wants you to smile today. Now, what about the future? We don't know what the future will bring, but we can learn from the woman

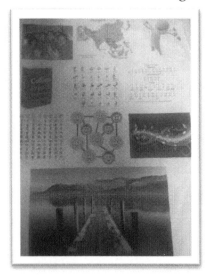

of noble character. The Bible says, *"Strength and dignity are her clothing, and she smiles at the future" (Proverbs 31:25).* I would say that the woman of noble character has a vision for what her life is and is to be. Do you?

Earlier I mentioned "Grab a Vision." Now let's see what this looks like:

In 2011, I was encouraged to make a visual map of my goals. I gave myself freedom to dream, and I made this map you see on this page. The pictures represents freedom, music, wide open horizons, traveling, learning a new language, connecting with new people, and teaching students from another country. I didn't know at the time what I wanted to do, and I was encouraged to make a visual map of pictures that would help me to have vision for my life in the next years. Very shockingly, a year later I looked at this map and I was sitting in my paid apartment in South Korea, loving my life, connected with new people, teaching wonderful students, playing music with bands in the area, learning the language, and crying tears of joy, visiting children in need, finding myself used by the Lord by His grace, and being more free in Him than I have ever felt before! Wow! God told Abraham, *"Look at the stars and count them if you can. So shall your offspring be" (Genesis 15:5).*

We need to dream. God has placed a dream in all of our hearts. Don't be afraid to dream and take practical steps to moving in that direction. We need to grab a vision. We were not made to be mundane, not one of us. We were made with dreams in our hearts. We were made to walk in that direction. What is God impressing on your heart to visualize today?

I would encourage you, all that God has given you is there right now inside of you. Yes, right now you can write down the dream and make it clear so that people can see it and understand it (see Habakkuk 2:2). It takes courage, though. Won't you be courageous today? Share your dreams, your vision, and your goals with somebody today. God is not against you. He is for you. Take the time to visualize the things you want out of life. Don't be shy. Trust what God has given inside you. Do not suppress it. If you deny it, it is still there. Write it down. No one else can tell you your dream; it has to come from you.

I'm praying God's greatest, His great and mighty blessings over your life and in the lives of those around you today.

Epiphany #23: Today is your Debut!

If you have a DVD lying around, take a look at the deleted scenes sometime and notice one thing. Simply observe the way the actors are acting. While creating a film, do you think the actors in the movie know which scenes from the movie will be in the deleted scenes, and which ones won't make it? I think it's fair to say, generally, "No." In theory, any scene could be a box office smash.

What is my point? We often go through our lives thinking that today will be one of our deleted scenes, and we think that one of those days in the distant future will be our box office smash part. Let me tell you, when actors perform, they perform their very best in each and every scene, not knowing which will be the one that will make the movie. Our lives are similar to this analogy. I believe sometimes we act like most of our lives are just a full set of movie scenes that don't and won't matter. We treat today like it's going to be a deleted scene is our number one selling movie. But, our lives are not a conglomeration of deleted scenes. That said, we all need to see how dearly we need to act as though every scene in our life is our debut scene. Each scene matters.

Do not start pre-editing your scenes. Stop pre-determining which scenes are deleted scenes in your life. We do not and cannot fully know which parts in our lives are important and which ones aren't; which actors in your movie are important and which ones aren't. That's God's job. Your job is to simply perform and be your best you. Let God do the editing. Just remember: every moment of your life is your debut. So envision every moment with you as fully the one that God made you to be. He made you to be ALIVE! Smile, you're on camera, so never tire of doing what is good (see 2 Thessalonians 3:13)!

Epiphany #24: What do you want your new recording album to sound like?

Since we established ourselves as actors, might as well be singers, too! Okay, so if you could record an album that would reach millions and millions of listeners, what would you want your album to sound like? What would be the name of your album? What would be your message? Let's think about this further. When a singer records a new album, he or she pays careful attention to the lyrics they use and the kinds of songs they will put out there for the world to hear. They also pay close attention to the order of the songs on the album because they want their audience to have an experience. They want them to understand the flow and the theme of the entire album so their audience gets the best impact from their experience listening to that album.

So now, think of your new life, everything you do, and every word that you say like the lyrics to the songs of your latest recording album. Think of one person with whom you frequently speak. This person is like an audience of a million because, as we know, people have had impacts that can multiply by just talking with one person. The point here is not to release an album that reaches millions and millions just because. The point here is to get a firm understanding of what message is that we are sending out into the world every single day. Have you ever considered what message you want people to receive from your life? Because, whether we want to or not, that is exactly what we are doing every single day.

Before we go on to describe your recording album, let's consider this: the majority of us tend to sell ourselves so very short. We value others on television and on Youtube, but we don't value ourselves or the things we have to say. This is not helpful. Again, I don't mean the kind of value that is self-centered or void of God's presence. I mean the kind of value that says, "I am a child of the Most High and my Father is the Maker of all things." Once more, like David, I mean the kind of value in yourself and in God that makes you say to your big giant, *"You come against me with sword and spear and javelin, but I come against you in the name of the LORD Almighty, the God of the armies of Israel, whom you have defied. This day the LORD will deliver you into my hands, and I'll strike you down and cut off your head. This very day I will give the carcasses of the Philistine army to the birds and the wild animals, and the whole world will know that there is a God in Israel"* (1 Samuel 17:45-46). This is the kind of value we need to have in our lives. So what do you want your new recording album to look and sound like? Let's get more detailed about this.

As I mentioned, each day you release a new album and you promote it to others. At most, probably there's a list of the top 12 phrases you'll give to the people around you. Let's call this your song list from your album. These songs, the phrases you give as you go about the day, are your theme. So what is your theme? This can be summed up in one title from your heart: your Album Name. Go ahead and write down what you want the name of your most recent album, life album, and twelve phrases to be. We are all listening.

Here is a sample of my own:

Theme: Show others the awesomeness and love of God through Christ Jesus

Song 1: God is awesome!

Song 2: God is great!

Song 3: Love my wife

Song 4: Love my children and my family

Song 5: Show kindness to others

Song 6: Show impact within your community

Song 7: I can do all things through Christ Who strengthens me.

Song 8: Smile and laugh more

Song 9: Be still and know that He alone is God

Song 10: Praise the Lord!

Song 11: Give praise to God and worship the LORD with all your heart!

Song 12: O how sweet is the name above all names, how sweet is the name JESUS

Chapter Nine

Smile on Purpose

Epiphany #25: Be deliberate about your life

So be deliberate about life. Think of these questions: What words do you want to be synonymous with you? What products? What clothing? Be intentional about yourself and life. I'm not trying to get you to sell yourself to people. I'm trying to get you to BE yourself, intentionally, before God and people.

Whether you like it or not, you are advertising your own theme everywhere you go all the time anyway! What are all the things that you are portraying in your life right now, and what do you want them to be? Maybe it is that you are redeemed! So what does that look like? Maybe it is that you are victorious in Christ! That you are more than a conqueror! That you go from glory to glory. So what does that look like? Maybe you just think you are a mess...well find me the scripture and I'll let you off the hook...but seriously, look in the Bible and discover how God sees you. Because of His

Conclusion

Why a book on God wanting us to smile? I felt like writing this book because there are far too many, including myself, who think that God does not want them to smile; that He is not a smiling Ruler of the universe. I secretly thought that God didn't want the best for me. I wouldn't admit this before, but I secretly thought that God was full of hate; a Ruler who expresses delight was far from my imagination. To me it sounded funny, or even strange, that God smiled; so I wrote this book.

Sometimes I looked at the Bible and never perceived God as smiling at me, and therefore I didn't think that God wanted me to really smile. I justified my feelings by looking for other Christians who felt guilty when they smiled. I felt comfortable around Christians who felt like they shouldn't...or at least they should do something to make up for the times they genuinely do smile because that is me! If the people who claimed to be Christians were caught actually enjoying their lives, I would secretly think something was wrong with them! How dare they listen to that music! How dare they make that much money! AND ENJOY IT! How dare they smile and not repent later for it! I know what you are thinking – what a jerk! But that was me! I thought sinners enjoyed their lives and that saints struggled and go through all kinds of pains. Which is true sometimes, but not all the time. And that is the difference.

But God is smacking me in the face and telling me it makes a difference when you believe and know that God's purpose is that He, the God of all the universe, your Father, wants all of His children to smile. What makes you smile? I believe He wants us to experience and to be able to express joy unspeakable in His name. He wants all of His children to enjoy life every day. My prayer is that this book will not only make you smile, but it will also give you a fresh awakened outlook on your everyday life, your destiny, and the great impact you can and will make on others around you.

My prayer for you is that you will take it upon yourself to make your smile a part of your mission. I pray that today you may take full responsibility for your own smile. I pray that we will smile at how great our God is, and how good God is daily, and that we will shine with all the radiance of God Himself as we love others with genuine love and with a warming heart of concern for those God brings in our path.

I pray that our character grows and that people all around us will notice. I pray that we will no longer be afraid or timid, but be so filled with the love, joy, and peace that only comes from the LORD, and that we share it with all those in our circle.

"I pray that in every way you may prosper and enjoy good health, as your soul also prospers." 3 John 1:2

"I pray that out of his glorious riches [God] may strengthen you with power through his Spirit in your inner being, so that Christ may dwell in your hearts through faith. And I pray that you, being rooted and established in love, may have power, together with all the Lord's holy people, to grasp how wide and long and high and deep is the love of Christ, and to know this love that surpasses knowledge — that you may be filled to the measure of all the fullness of God. Ephesians 3:16-19

Genuine laughter and smiling are of the genius of God

Take a minute and close your eyes, thinking about how you will make your best friends, your family, and others you know smile.

I have a challenge for you: If you have an idea that you can see will make someone smile with delight, don't delay - do it! Don't do it for money. Do it because of the joy it will bring. I know that this is what is motivating me to get this book out to you! All you need is all you have now. What you do by principle gives more, gives back, and is a blessing to both you and the people around you. We were made to make other people joyful with our talents. We were made to make other people smile. Welcome to the smile revolution. ☺

Jesus is God's eternal smile, smiling on us.

"In the beginning was the Word. The Word was with God, and the Word was God. He was with God in the beginning." Everything came into existence through him. Not one thing that exists was made without him . . . He was the source of life, and that life was the light for humanity. The light shines in the dark, and the dark has never extinguished it." John 1:1-5

"The Word became human and lived among us. We saw his glory. It was the glory that the Father shares with his only Son, a glory full of kindness and truth."
John 1:14

At a time when darkness was all that seemed to be around. During a time when confusion, frustration, and quietness was taking place, the light of the world came in. The light of the world is coming into your life today. Jesus came into this world to settle it once and for all that God IS INDEED smiling on you right now. *"For God did not send his son into the world to condemn the world, but to save it" (John 3:17).* It is settled. God does not hate you nor does He look upon you with ANY form of distain whatsoever. God loves you and wants more for you than you could ever imagine in your entire lifetime. Won't you trust Him today? Let's pray this prayer together, but before we do, I want you to tell me about this prayer if you've prayed it from your heart, okay? Let's pray:

Dear Father, I know you love me. Please forgive me of my sin. I know that I am a sinner who needs you. Lord, I know you are smiling on me, not because of my sin, but because I am your (son or daughter). Father, I accept your forgiveness of my sin, and I now accept your free gift of eternal life through your one and only Son, Jesus Christ. I accept Jesus as LORD over my life today! I am now a new creation! I am made whole! I am changed! My life is blessed and I am NEVER going back! In Jesus' Mighty Holy Awesome and Marvelous Name, I pray! Amen! And Amen!

It is done. Congratulations! You are a now and forever a child of The Most High God! God is with you. He is for you. And you will be a blessing to the nations, PERIOD.

As I said, please share with me your prayer and I would love to hear from you. Thank you for taking this smiling adventure with me, and may God bless you and keep you. May the Lord smile on you and be so kind to you, may He look on you with love mercy and favor, and grant you His peace (see Numbers 24-26).

God bless you.

Made in the USA
Columbia, SC
23 September 2018